Coloring Book For Seniors

Nature Designs Vol 1

ART THERAPY COLORING

Preview of Coloring Pages

Preview of Coloring Pages

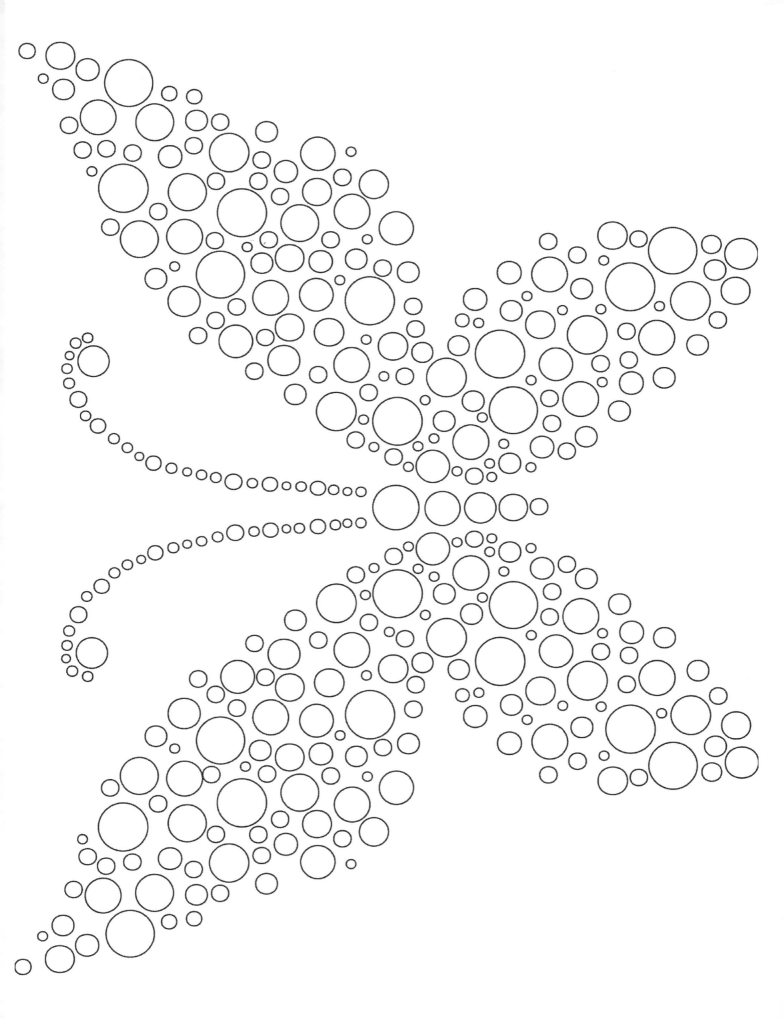

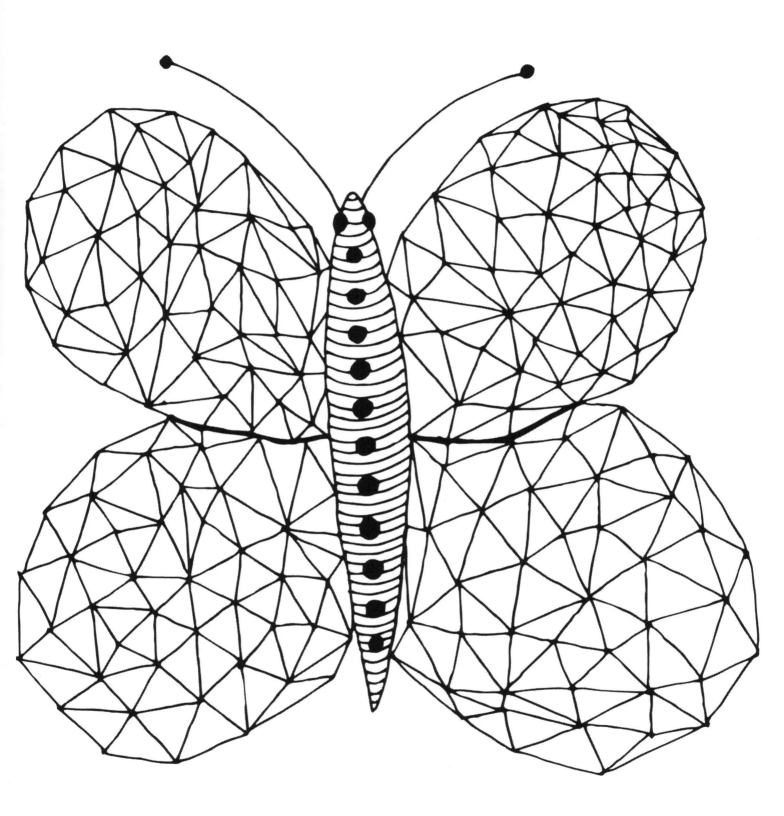

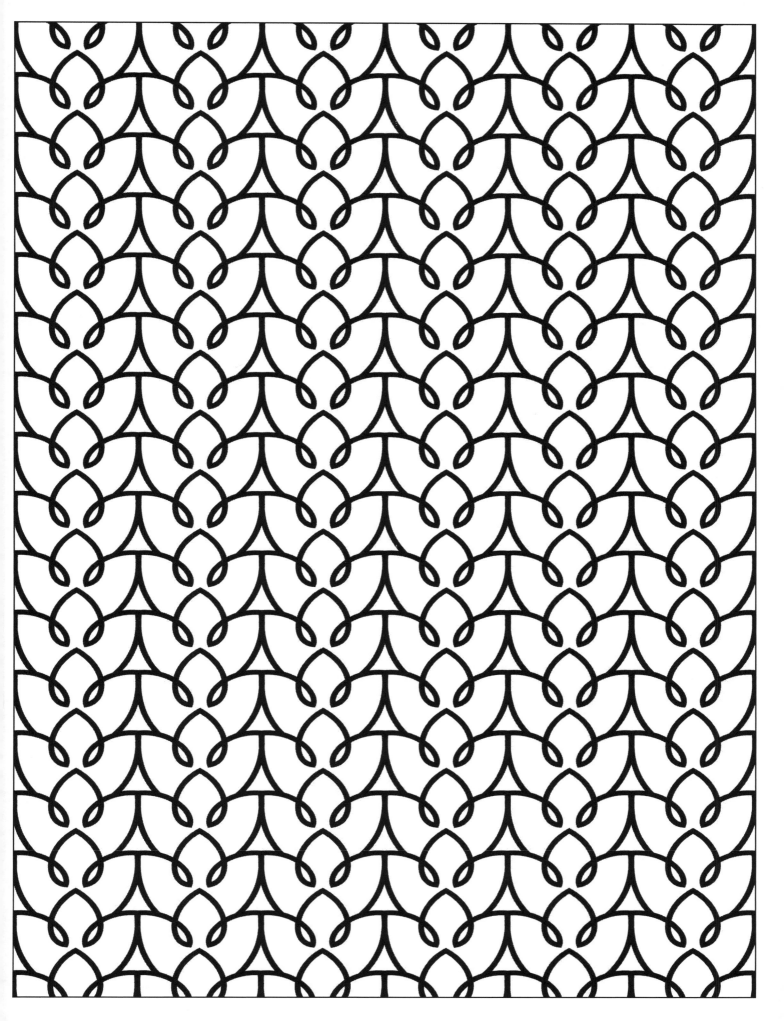

Did You Enjoy Our Coloring Book?

We Want To Hear About It!

Help spread the word about our coloring books! The best way to spread the word is through reviews. We know how busy you are, especially with all of that coloring, but we would appreciate it!

Visit our website at www.arttherapycoloring.com

Over 200 Art Therapy Coloring Books

See our collection of over 200 Art Therapy Coloring Books for Adults, Men, Women, Seniors, Teens, Kids, Boys, and Girls.

Coloring Books For Seniors

Coloring Book For Seniors
Anti-Stress Designs Vol 1
ART THERAPY COLORING

Coloring Book For Seniors
Nature Designs Vol 1
ART THERAPY COLORING

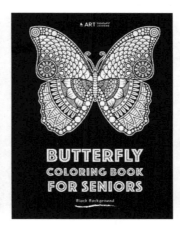

BUTTERFLY
COLORING BOOK
FOR SENIORS
Black Background
ART THERAPY COLORING

COLORING BOOKS
FOR SENIORS
ANIMAL DESIGNS

MANDALA
COLORING BOOK
FOR SENIORS

MANDALA
COLORING BOOK
FOR SENIORS
Black Background

COLORING BOOKS
FOR SENIORS
HEART DESIGNS
ART THERAPY COLORING

HAPPY
BIRTHDAY!

HAPPY BIRTHDAY
TO YOU ON YOUR
70TH BIRTHDAY
Black Background

COLORING BOOKS
FOR SENIORS
SWIRL DESIGNS
Black Background

COLORING BOOKS
FOR SENIORS
RELAXING DESIGNS
ART THERAPY COLORING

Coloring Book For Seniors
Anti-Stress Designs Vol 2
ART THERAPY COLORING

Coloring Book For Seniors
Anti-Stress Designs Vol 3
ART THERAPY COLORING

Coloring Book For Seniors
Anti-Stress Designs Vol 4
ART THERAPY COLORING

Coloring Book For Seniors
Floral Designs Vol 1
ART THERAPY COLORING

live
simply

Coloring Book For Seniors
Floral Designs Vol 2
ART THERAPY COLORING

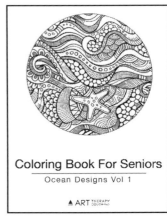

Coloring Book For Seniors
Ocean Designs Vol 1
ART THERAPY COLORING

Coloring Books For Adults

ZOMBIE
COLORING BOOK
Black Background

ZOMBIES
COLORING BOOK
SCARY DESIGNS
Black Background

DRAGON
COLORING BOOK

DRAGON
COLORING BOOK
Black Background

AFRICA
COLORING BOOK
FOR ADULTS

LION
COLORING BOOK
FOR ADULTS

TIGER
COLORING BOOK
FOR ADULTS

WILD ANIMALS
COLORING BOOK
ZENDOODLE DESIGNS

UNICORN
ADULT COLORING BOOKS
Black Background

HORSE
COLORING BOOK
DETAILED DESIGNS

HORSE
COLORING BOOKS
FOR ADULTS
Black Background

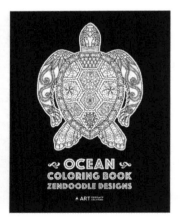

OCEAN
COLORING BOOK
ZENDOODLE DESIGNS

WOLF
COLORING BOOK
FOR ADULTS

DOG
COLORING BOOK
DOODLE DESIGNS

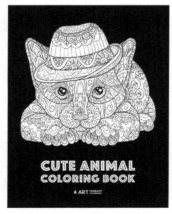

CUTE ANIMAL
COLORING BOOK

CUTE CAT
COLORING BOOK

Coloring Books For Adults

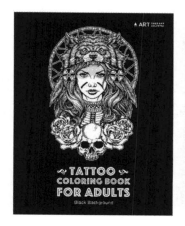

TATTOO
COLORING BOOK
FOR ADULTS
Black Background

TATTOO
COLORING BOOK
FOR ADULTS

TATTOO
COLORING BOOK
FOR ADULTS RELAXATION

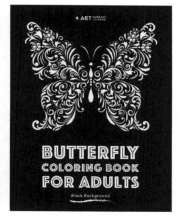

BUTTERFLY
COLORING BOOK
FOR ADULTS
Black Background

NATIVE AMERICAN
COLORING BOOK
FOR ADULTS

COLORING BOOKS
FOR ADULTS
RELAXATION
Native American Inspired Designs

SKULL
COLORING BOOK
FOR ADULTS

SWIRLS
COLORING BOOK
FOR ADULTS
Black Background

DOG & COFFEE
COLORING BOOK
FOR ADULTS

CAT & COFFEE
COLORING BOOK
FOR ADULTS

INTRICATE
COLORING BOOK
FOR ADULTS VOL 2

INTRICATE
COLORING BOOK
FOR ADULTS VOL 5

OCEAN
COLORING BOOK
FOR ADULTS

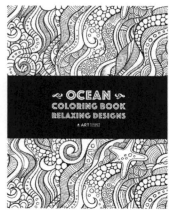

OCEAN
COLORING BOOK
RELAXING DESIGNS

PATTERNS
COLORING BOOK
FOR ADULTS
Black Background

FISHING

FISHING
COLORING BOOK
FOR ADULTS
Black Background

Coloring Books For Adults

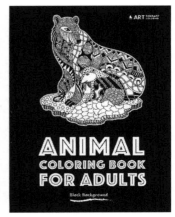

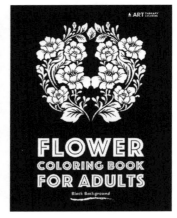

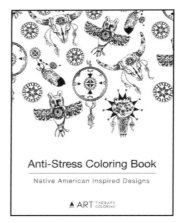

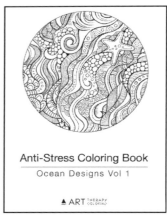

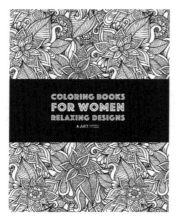

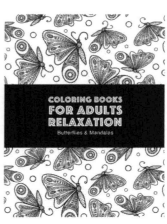

Coloring Books For Men

Coloring Book For Men
Anti-Stress Designs Vol 1

COLORING BOOK
FOR MEN
ANIMAL DESIGNS

COLORING BOOKS
FOR MEN
HUNTING

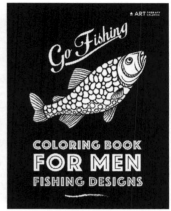

Go Fishing
COLORING BOOK
FOR MEN
FISHING DESIGNS

COLORING BOOK
FOR MEN
BIKER DESIGNS

COLORING BOOK
FOR MEN
SKULL DESIGNS
Black Background

COLORING BOOK
FOR MEN
TATTOO DESIGNS
Black Background

ADULT
COLORING BOOK FOR MEN
ANIMAL DESIGNS
Black Background

ANIMAL
COLORING BOOK
FOR SENIORS MEN

NATURE
COLORING BOOK
FOR SENIORS MEN

OCEAN
COLORING BOOK
FOR SENIORS MEN

COLORING BOOK
FOR MEN
HAPPY BIRTHDAY
Black Background

Coloring Books For Teens

COLORING BOOKS
FOR TEENS
WOLVES & MORE

TEEN
COLORING BOOKS
ANIMAL DESIGNS

TEEN
COLORING BOOKS
ANIMALS
Black Background

COLORING BOOKS
FOR TEENS
OWLS

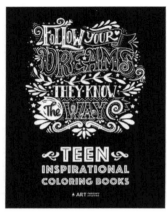

TEEN
INSPIRATIONAL
COLORING BOOKS

TEEN
COLORING BOOKS
ANIMAL DESIGNS
Black Background

DETAILED
COLORING BOOK
FOR TEENAGERS
Animal Designs

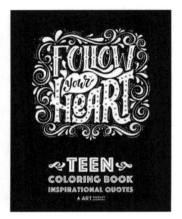

TEEN
COLORING BOOK
INSPIRATIONAL QUOTES

TWEEN COLORING
BOOKS FOR GIRLS
CUTE ANIMALS

ADULT COLORING BOOKS
FOR TEENS
Animal Designs

COLORING BOOKS
FOR TEENS
CAT & DOG DESIGNS

MANDALA
COLORING BOOK
FOR TEENS
Black Background

COLORING BOOKS
FOR TEENS
SEAHORSES & MORE

COLORING BOOKS
FOR TEENS
RELAXATION
Dolphins & More

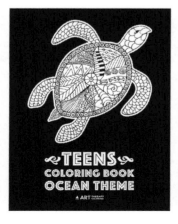

TEENS
COLORING BOOK
OCEAN THEME

COLORING BOOKS
FOR TEENS
SHARKS & MORE

Coloring Books For Teens

Coloring Book For Teens
Anti-Stress Designs Vol 1

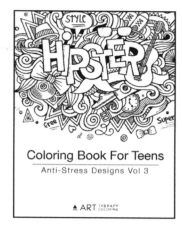

Coloring Book For Teens
Anti-Stress Designs Vol 2

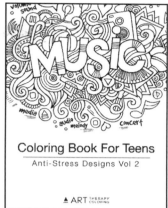

Coloring Book For Teens
Anti-Stress Designs Vol 3

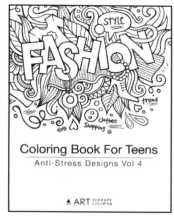

Coloring Book For Teens
Anti-Stress Designs Vol 4

Coloring Book For Teens
Anti-Stress Designs Vol 5

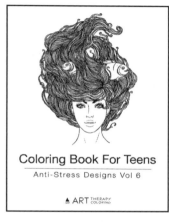

Coloring Book For Teens
Anti-Stress Designs Vol 6

Coloring Book For Teens
Anti-Stress Designs Vol 7

Coloring Book For Teens
Anti-Stress Designs Vol 8

GEOMETRIC COLORING BOOK FOR TEENS

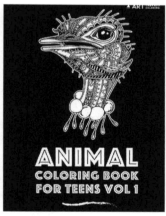

ANIMAL COLORING BOOK FOR TEENS VOL 1

ANIMAL COLORING BOOK FOR TEENS VOL 2

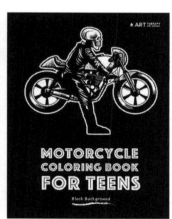

MOTORCYCLE COLORING BOOK FOR TEENS
Black Background

COLORING BOOKS FOR TEENS OCEAN DESIGNS

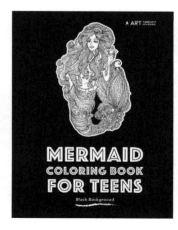

MERMAID COLORING BOOK FOR TEENS
Black Background

SKULL COLORING BOOK FOR TEENS
Black Background

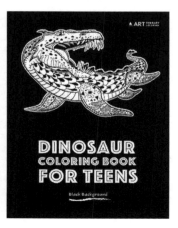

DINOSAUR COLORING BOOK FOR TEENS
Black Background

Coloring Books For Girls

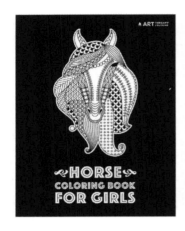

HORSE
COLORING BOOK
FOR GIRLS

UNICORN
COLORING BOOK
FOR GIRLS

COLORING
BOOKS FOR GIRLS
UNICORNS

COLORING BOOKS
FOR GIRLS
ANIMAL DESIGNS

COLORING BOOKS
FOR TEEN GIRLS VOL 1
DETAILED DESIGNS

TEEN
COLORING BOOKS
FOR GIRLS VOL 1

TEEN
COLORING BOOKS
FOR GIRLS VOL 2

TEEN
COLORING BOOKS
FOR GIRLS VOL 3

COLORING
BOOKS FOR GIRLS
CUTE ANIMALS

GIRLS
COLORING BOOKS
CUTE ANIMALS

COLORING
BOOKS FOR GIRLS
ANIMALS

COLORING BOOKS
FOR GIRLS
Princess & Unicorn Designs

GIRLS
COLORING BOOKS
DETAILED DESIGNS VOL 1

GIRLS
COLORING BOOKS
DETAILED DESIGNS VOL 2

with
LOVE

GIRLS
COLORING BOOKS
DETAILED DESIGNS VOL 2

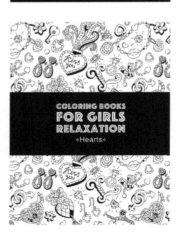

COLORING BOOKS
FOR GIRLS
RELAXATION
Hearts

Art Therapy Coloring Books

COLORING BOOKS
FOR TEEN GIRLS
DETAILED DESIGNS

Black Background

TEEN GIRLS
COLORING BOOKS
DETAILED DESIGNS

Native American Inspired

COLORING BOOKS
FOR TEENS
RELAXATION

Nature Designs

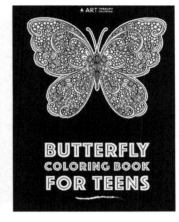

BUTTERFLY
COLORING BOOK
FOR TEENS

COLORING BOOKS
FOR TEEN GIRLS VOL 2
DETAILED DESIGNS

ADULT
COLORING BOOKS
FOR GIRLS

Detailed Designs

COLORING BOOKS
FOR GIRLS
DETAILED DESIGNS VOL 1

COLORING BOOKS
FOR GIRLS
OCEAN DESIGNS

COLORING BOOKS
FOR GIRLS
RELAXATION

Black Background

COLORING BOOKS
FOR OLDER KIDS
GEOMETRIC DESIGNS

HEART
COLORING BOOK
FOR KIDS

DETAILED
COLORING BOOKS
FOR KIDS

Ocean Designs

ANIMAL
COLORING BOOK
FOR OLDER KIDS

COLORING BOOKS
FOR OLDER KIDS
ANIMAL DESIGNS

COLORING BOOKS
FOR GIRLS
RELAXATION

Butterflies

BUTTERFLY
COLORING BOOK
FOR KIDS

Detailed Designs

Coloring Books For Boys

COLORING BOOKS
FOR BOYS
WILD ANIMALS
ART THERAPY COLORING

COLORING BOOKS
FOR BOYS
~DRAGONS~
ART THERAPY COLORING

COLORING BOOKS
FOR BOYS
ANIMAL DESIGNS
ART THERAPY COLORING

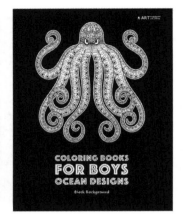

COLORING BOOKS
FOR BOYS
OCEAN DESIGNS
Black Background

COLORING BOOKS
FOR BOYS
~SHARKS~
ART THERAPY COLORING

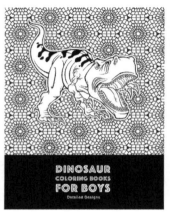

DINOSAUR
COLORING BOOKS
FOR BOYS
Detailed Designs

COLORING BOOKS
FOR BOYS
NATIVE AMERICAN INSPIRED
ART THERAPY COLORING

COLORING
BOOKS FOR BOYS
ANIMALS
ART THERAPY COLORING

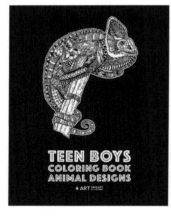

TEEN BOYS
COLORING BOOK
ANIMAL DESIGNS
ART THERAPY COLORING

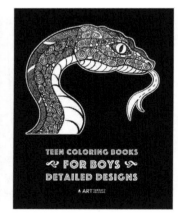

TEEN COLORING BOOKS
~FOR BOYS~
DETAILED DESIGNS
ART THERAPY COLORING

TEEN COLORING BOOKS
~FOR BOYS~
DETAILED DESIGNS
Black Background

COLORING BOOKS
FOR TEEN BOYS
DETAILED DESIGNS
ART THERAPY COLORING

COLORING BOOKS
FOR TEEN BOYS
DETAILED DESIGNS
Black Background

ADULT
COLORING BOOKS
FOR KIDS
Geometric Designs

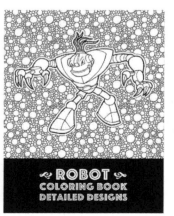

~ROBOT~
COLORING BOOK
DETAILED DESIGNS

DETAILED
COLORING BOOKS
FOR KIDS
Geometric Designs

Coloring Books For Kids

DETAILED
COLORING BOOKS
FOR KIDS
Zoo Animals

COLORING BOOKS
FOR KIDS AGES 8-12
~ANIMALS~
Black Background

DETAILED
COLORING BOOKS
FOR KIDS

~ZOMBIE~
COLORING BOOK
FOR KIDS

DETAILED
COLORING BOOKS
FOR KIDS
~Animals~

DETAILED
COLORING BOOKS
FOR KIDS
~Elephants~

COLORING BOOKS
FOR KIDS
OCEAN DESIGNS

MANDALA
COLORING BOOK
FOR KIDS
Black Background

DETAILED
COLORING BOOKS
FOR KIDS
~Butterflies~

~UNICORN~
COLORING BOOK
FOR KIDS AGES 4-8
Volume 1

~UNICORN~
COLORING BOOK
FOR KIDS AGES 4-8
Volume 2

COLORING
BOOKS FOR KIDS
CUTE ANIMALS

~KIDS~
MANDALA
COLORING BOOK

MANDALA
COLORING BOOK
FOR KIDS

~SHARK~
COLORING BOOK

DINOSAUR
COLORING BOOK

Coloring Books For Special Occasions

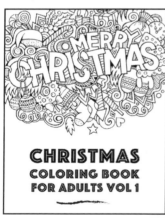

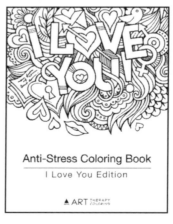

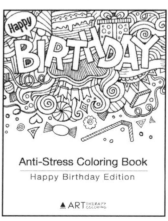

Coloring Book For Seniors
Nature Designs Vol 1

Published by:
Art Therapy Coloring
El Dorado Hills, California
www.arttherapycoloring.com

ISBN: 978-1-944427-40-5

6663649JR00050

Made in the USA
Columbia, SC
18 July 2019